T0266092

In the Builded Place

POEMS BY MICHAEL HELLER

COFFEE HOUSE PRESS :: MINNEAPOLIS :: 1989

These poems appeared often in slightly different forms in the following magazines: *Harpers, Bluefish, SUN, Conjunctions, Pequod, The Ohio Review, Images, New Letters, Occurrence, American Poetry Review, Ninth Decade* (England), *Montemora, Boundary 2, Occident, New York Poetry, Frank, Margin,* and *Talisman.*

"Statue: Jardin Du Luxemborg", "On a Line from Baudelaire", "Outside a Classroom in Nerja", "For Uncle Nat" previously appeared in a chapbook entitled MARGINALIA IN A DESPERATE HAND published as No. 9 of a series in the STAPLE DIET chapbooks by Pig Press (Durham, England).

"Father Studies" was included in CAPSTAN, an anthology of poems by recipients of the N.Y. State Fellowships in Poetry. "Coral Stanzas" and "Two Swans In A Meadow By The Sea" appeared in the anthology *Long Island Poets.* "For Uncle Nat" appeared in the *Survey of American Poetry.*

Copyright © 1989 by Michael Heller.
Cover art by Kate Van Cleve.
Back cover photo by Jane Augustine.

The publisher thanks the National Endowment for the Arts, Cowles Media/Star Tribune, and Dayton Hudson, for support for this book.

Coffee House Press books are distributed to trade by CONSORTIUM BOOK SALES AND DISTRIBUTION, 287 East Sixth Street Suite 365, Saint Paul, Minnesota 55101. For personal orders, catalogs or other information, write to:
COFFEE HOUSE PRESS
27 NORTH FOURTH STREET, SUITE 400, MINNEAPOLIS, MN 55401.

Library of Congress Cataloging in Publication Data
Heller, Michael, 1937-
        In the builded place : poems / by Michael Heller.
            p. cm.
    ISBN 0-918273-58-7
    I. Title.
PS3558.E476215   1989
811'.54 – dc20   89-27273   CIP

Contents

In Memory, Pete and Martha

&

for Jane and Tena and Nicholas

"Circles and right lines limit and close all bodies, and the mortall right-lined circle (θ The Character of Death) must conclude and shut up all."

— SIR THOMAS BROWNE, *Urn Burial*

I

WITH A TELESCOPE IN THE
SANGRE DE CRISTOS

There
Where the mountains bulked
Above the valley floor

And town and ranch lights
Made shallow bowls
Into other heavens

Raw nature actually seemed less raw.

Again and again that night
The glass checked
In its round frame

The nebula's thumbprint swirls:
This fine life of bonds and connections…

Then
I looked in
At another's eyes

Looked past that image
Of the self,
In at the pupil's black hole

Where light gives up
The granular,
Becomes a maelstrom

Grinding
Beyond the phenomenal
To a lightless, frightening depth.

O this fine life of bonds and connections…

FATHER PARMENIDES

Neither great nor small
The hollow simply is.

Like the wine of its cask, the voice
Empties the speaker, empties
Even the void at fullness.

MOON STUDY

To steal a look at it as the tide pulls,
And the earth, sheathed in the living
And non-living, bulges and dimples

At the surface of the seas. The moon!
It appears beyond my capacity
To do more than give it name, to shout

Like the haiku master, O bright!
O bright! O moon! as though
With a word I could embrace

some lucent teaching of its being. To have
No hold on this architect of shadows, this
Realm of space, of airless peaks, fantastical…

America, tranquil and monumental under
the hard moon, is also a dream of cold light
Raining purity of cities alabaster.

And now, sister of the obdurate,
How the body of love gleams otherworldly,
Exotic with distance and intimacy. O pallid!

O nightmares of wars and terrors, O terrible
Bright! The great pocked surfaces,
Craters of the moon, craters of the bomb,

These two texts have swallowed *cri de coeur,*
Ode and epistle, our books of loss.
In the restless night, at the window,
My white ego meets that white eye.

CORAL STANZAS

— after Mandelstam

O city, O white filagree just below the grainy depths.
Can it be a reef which absorbs the star and moonlight?
O reef, am I flung, cast toward shoal, toward beach?
Is there water clear enough, soothes enough,
Surrounding the far-flung branchings?

Bitumin pellicles fester in the vision,
Falling like hell-snow, falling like hell-snow.
O into depths, more depths, your brother animal
Swims into poisoned channels.

Brother animal. O white filagree, city of Venus.
Light mote and tear duct festering in the hell-snow,
In the scurried depths.

THE BRIGHT LIGHT AT THE POINT

to G. O.

Read the words of the African tribe
on the civilizing of the world:
"this earth has lines upon its face,
scoured marks upon its ground"

and walk in this
eye-piercing light,

the sky a guillotine of blue,
world severed into edges:
water, shore, two houses on their separate dunes.

And I am cleaved, lined, marked off
against the century and its full-
blown dreams, its fantasy of control
as though the world were caught
within the body,
and every thought or hope swam
locked within the oily mass.

Cicatrice sadness here,
where, way off, bells and buoys
cast their lonely moans into the open space,

for the light — this modern light — is piteous,
sheering and estranging clarity

lest each one shipwreck on one's self.

AT BEACHES AGAIN

I.
To have heard:
Indians made escape routes
Through this dense cover of gnarled pines,
Paths snaking under matted poison ivy
To emerge in sunlight brilliant enough to cleanse.

To arrive at this beach
Where Marconi set up his wireless
Among the dunes. Foregrounded

Before the sea, three blistered iron struts
Bolted to a concrete base, rust flakes
And stripped nuts scarred by the wrench.

The long bleached stretch of sand
Is not unlike Kitty Hawk further south
Where the Wrights launched and the Indians there

Had long since

II.
Lovely, these spots
Where waves come in, go out,
And the clouds are banked at the horizon

Like another mass of coast.
The sky then adrift,
And one can imagine messages,

Signals, as we now signal stars,
Coalescing out of salt-washed air:
An unseen human tincture

Of news reports of them
'dying over there.'
We, in our own way, of course, are dying,

But there are many ways to die,
To come back, to survive
Our incontinent desires and wars, many ways

To re-enter certain deeps, though
We taint even the run-off of continents
And make of this ocean

Something more than witness,
Make of it a communicant.

III.
Imagine, as he said, "the light
holding for an instant..."
Enough to make one get in the car,

Drive out to that bluff above
The bay's sweep, to find
The view so magnificent, truly

No one need be standing in it.
And the little world of the head
Is brained like a drum

Against this lightswept other,
Is suddenly error
Fallen out of time,

Vague solipsism
to the counterpoint
of the foam-tipped sway of waves.

And the beach edge bakes in sun, the space
Suggesting endless stupefying lethargy.
There, a coiled rope, a drawn-up boat,

Signs human but also of the sea.

IV.
Times when the jukebox true?
That fractious music!
When the sentiment is free

And the heart goes for nothing
Toward some extravagance of words,
Times which obsess us and our disappointments

Are terrible. We have come to the time
Of the accurate missile, of concern for such
Accuracy in the world, of all that we call terror.

Even love is poised on that pelvic
Terror, on the wave and its sparkling foam
One barely hears in the world.

We have yet to hear that wave break,
Hoping we are shoreward enough
But that we are overheard.

For speech, speech comes with ease to us,
Yet what if there is more of that wave in man
Than speech.

V
In the classics, man was added to nature
To make an art both bitter and sweet,
An art not good for us who stand here.

This cliff edge leads outward
Towards the deepest blues of space,
Worlds of history at one's back —

The dead and wasted centuries.
And here one can manipulate the gaze
So that the gazer finds himself expendable.

Hölderlin spoke of these high

Marine lookouts where no one wants to be.
And Lorca, as a child,

Would walk into the sea
Only with his back to the waves.

The last sense here
Is the sense of taking leave.

VI.
Woods into which the Indians fled,
Dark as a closed book or the death-flecks
That cling to the mind's sheer open

Brilliance. And the wet black kelp strung
Along the sand is already maidenhair,
Dragging the eye down, vectoring
Towards the waves, away from the light.

And the beach is wide, wide to the water
And swept by winds. Possibly a bird
Marks fresh tracks over the dune's ripple,

The spiky shadow of the weed
Scythes even this brightness.

THE ACOUSTICS OF EMPTINESS

What the ceiling absorbs.
Possibly that which I don't want to hear.
Noise over hollow, over self-abyss, chatter
That clucks I'm a chicken before the axe falls.
Anxious, I believe it. The nerves are a lush playing field,
A gaggle of neurons, well-tended in the pilot,
Swathed in the formal blankets of discourse in the diplomat.
Yet what I hear is the mind-forged mumblings of tyrants:
"flowers," "democracy," "he's human" — that's chatter!
The panelling with its punched holes holding the hearsay,
The old cliches of the poem, like worshipping silence.

IN THE BUILDED PLACE

"I wandered thro' each charter'd street"
— B L A K E

In the unfair life
Of this night or any other,
In this city,

Someone's broken world,
In the streetlamp's
Small circle of light,

To find no magic aura, no blaze
Of clarity on the broken littered pavement,
To find neither justice

Nor penance of lives, to find
Only the absurd arrangements and disarrangements:
A slum block in the light's cool bath of truth.

*

Who will it hurt that tonight
This broken world is but a literal?
Who will it hurt to note

The light on a woman's face?
To see her face pend in time?
Can it hurt to note

The weight of time
Weighing down the lovely features,
Unable to break loose

From that which it weighs upon.
It suggests no more than you resolve this:
The gross weight of life in time

Looking to be resolved in meaning,
Solved in love.

*

Tonight the clatter of failed myths,
Of hierarchies, dies. Tonight
We are joined as one in the street-lamp's light,

A corrosive light: dissolve, dissolve,
Discovering selves in the core of world,
That lonely need. So that we may arrive at last

In late dusk, in late time,
Bare islands of the human archipelago…
I stand back, watch the light on the curves

Of her face, not so much to feel
That rush of movement in me,
As to see again the quick and the alive

Open under open air.

*

And the sky's curve
Lies against the curve of the city.
Streets, people caught in thickness

Of event. And the eye and mind are led
To the moon's loft, to the bird aquiver,
To the serpent's gentle coil.

That they connect,
Connect like consciousness
In concentric whorls

Or like stations of the cross
Through loves, hates, errors…
These flimsy beatitudes of order.

ASTHMA

When the slight rasp in his throat starts up
My nuclear war-time goes interior, fills the whole head.
The shock-waved halfway house of hope de-domesticates to
    splinters.

The stores on the mall are so much bought hambone of desire,
Rorschachs of the mental wobblies, the local sales centers of sex,
Ingestion, *dégustation* flattening in the in-rush of punched air,

Uplifting the fear-bird's white wings, the smothering clutch
Of feathers that crams gullets. And the young boy
Whose sweet life is a keep, is my bank overdraft, my

Joy vault, he, who is not yet even historical, and so
Expends himself in file-throated shout, in play over
The junk-food city, the toy torture of the TV

That makes an idea as political as sliced pie
Or Psyche's credit-card sorting of seeds, laying
Down diet, health, avarice to store coin for

The dim video game of winter. And the child's
Cough, not the madman's speech, is so irrational, so contrary,
That black squander of air, that thick squalor

Where in this century most air is stolen.

WELL-DRESSING   ROUNDS*

— Ashford in the Water, Derbyshire

Terrorists leave notes
on dead bodies, warnings to others
not to touch, and I remember that Antigone,
against Creon's published male tyranny,
sought to set her brother's body to rights
not with other men but with the earth.
Possibly, the city man, out in England's
green fields, puts his hand to the grass
as though touching a pliant woman,
as though renewing a pact.

Here, in Ashford, flowers blaze,
bedeck the fields and woods.
And again, my hand sweeps as though
to gather this world to the fable book
where it once lived. But I'm a tourist,
with my own stories, walking
to the wellheads and to the bridge.

Last week, a printed handout tells us
school children gathered plants
and flowers among the trees,
pulled petals from blossoms,
plucked seeds from pod and husk,
gathered tufts of fur from rabbit pelts.
The teachers must have shown them how. I read,
and I'm with tourists, whose nations
divide up seas and lands while we walk
to wellheads and to the bridge.

Hands of children shaped
the crude, broad Marys and the Christs
with outstretched arms made of flower
upon part of flower, corn and pea
lining borders, all pressed
into now dried plaster. They ready

this bloodied world as though it were
a benison, *rise up o earth* —
the message as we talk and walk
round the basins of the wells.

Flowers are everywhere in Ashford.
It is midsummer; children dance the maypole
for visitors who come to walk the circuit
of the wells. Water rises up; it sparkles
in the sun, water of which we're made,
of which we drink, and this is what they honor
as we walk from the wellheads to the bridge.

* In certain towns in Derbyshire, the ancient wells are dressed
(decorated) each year during the period of the midsummer
solstice.

AFTER CLASS

Swirl, swirl, the leaves which Shelley summoned.
Dessicate the dead leaves across the park. Mr. Wolfgang,
Mr. Wolfgang has stopped me after class and dances, on
Toes, a dead leaf dance. And the bare trees are armature
Through which night descends. Who is in the park
But student, bum, tourist, visitor plastered like leaves
Against the dark. Mr. Wolfgang: "For fifty years I lived
In Berlin," and swirl begins. I look at Mr. Wolfgang's face,
But there is nothing that I ask. "I read," he says,
"that American's poem about a jar of glass. My head
Became that jar, so last year I came to *Co-net-e-cut!*
And now I'm here." Infectious swirl, infect swirl,
ja ja that jar. "Professor Heller, I must tell you
Something funny. I studied law for years. One of my
Professors made notes from another's book, then wrote
A book of his own. He did not know he wrote
The other professor's book. He was arrested."
Swirl, swirl. "It's so easy to get infected." Swirl.

I hear the dead leaves scrape my voice: history.

II

MYTHOS OF LOGOS

First the stars or the patterning of stars in darkness, and then perhaps someone climbing up a mountain to close the gap. Begins in dusty foothills, then forest, then high empty tundra and piles of rock, and at the top to brush at with the hand the spangled emptiness. But the hand feels nothing, sweeps nothing but the cold air. The loveliness of blackness for the first time brings solitude. And then one keeps silence at failure, nurses anger and shame, swallows the bitter taste.

And so the world becomes another place, and now I must confess to the many things that I forgot to say, was afraid to say, for fear, for love, for shame, O ancients and splendid hosts whose words come before and after,

Who have uttered out, one theory goes, what was written in the gene codes and in the stars' imprints before our speech. And now, those lucid structures are gantries to my nights, wheeling and reassembling.

And yes the whole career is night, is crafted out of silence. And so the sentences out there were not unsaid, nor did they blow away with stellar dust and stellar time. They settled down about my head, resembling a dome the exact shape of my skull hidden from others by a flap of skin.

AFTER PLATO

To the poet: not to be original.
No heart can fully voice itself.
No public so bemused to follow.

How to bear a poem whose truth
Would sear the sky, a bright sun
Rising per schedule. More heat,

More sweat, more guilt to add
To toil? Poet, spend your days
Surmising cloud banks of which

There are a vast sufficiency.
Praise occluded forms:
Your blinded loves, your hates.

Too dull? Too milky in their lucence?
Think of horrors when in the calm
Someone thought they saw the light.

Squint and wait for shifts of wind
To put shapes on chance maneuvers.
Ah, ruins afloat! See, your little

Nostalgia requires no contrastive blaze.
With luck, clouds will break
To rend familiars. This, the more-
Than-moment of the blinded reader.

As though, for you, a god
Had meant us sightless. As though
An eyelid had been peeled back
Only to insert a cinder.

HOMER TIMELESS

His way was not his way, but being blind
His way was that much more attuned to death.

Some called him camp-follower; others claimed
He justified Achilles' gloom, the tide of which
Had thrown down cities.

At the pyre, Achilles had Troy's twelve high-born
Slain. "This," the poet said, "was an evil thing."

Yet he also showed the bright blade's
Flashing beauty. He was accused:

He did not report the real war. The listener
Listens, remembers what he will remember.

*

It is said the wave-break off Hellas metronomes
His lines. What more noble than this mime of giving,

More honorable than to stay with his words
While outside, beyond the chair, is flesh and rubble.

Take the gift of his rhythms.

And after one is emptied by war, knots
Of one's stomach, nodules of ice, to imagine

Oneself among the maimed and rotting, the beach
Where once the sea was red with burning ships.

They could not go home. And while he spoke,
The Greece he spoke of made new Iliums

As newfound lands make new births.

RILKE'S SONG AT THE WINDOW

"Why am I weighed under this infinity?"

Depth-charged
Blossoming sea

Wanting force to surface
To bundle what's locked in:
Tensors, magnitudes, stripped nuclei
and burst them forth

And how clear one can draw lines:
To know I could not help you
And you bawling your head off

Into those shadows which were your past
And I searched myself to retrieve you
And I'd vomit up myself

And now I know the dead in life
—the dead we have brought with us—
And the stifled death of words are one

Terror is molecular:
That otherness we fought for
Was but this
virulence of ourselves

PHOTOGRAPH OF A MAN HOLDING HIS PENIS

for Michael Martone

World O world of the photograph, granular,
Quantumed for composition in the film's grain,
But here blurred, soft-toned and diffuse
Until the whole resolves into an ache, a
Chimerical, alchemical flower, a pattern
Against pure randomness.

As though the process itself exists to mock
What is discrete, is singular. Dot leans on dot,
On the binary of *only two* can make of one a life.

And the myth is partial,
A dream-half of need confused with desire.

I too live out this fear, this shadowed aloneness,
The white hand's delicate hold where the genital hairs
Are curled, the groin become a hermitage, a ghastly
Down of our featherings . . .

And the texture is bitter, bifurcate,
A braille of flesh
From which a ghost is sown.

TODAY, SOMEWHAT AFTER DANTE

The wind is blowing; the wind bends everything but the human will. Thus war and pillage have written more on the earth's surface than wind. The Wars, Vietnam, the Greater and Lesser Holocausts, these names, like those of the Florentine treacheries, season whatever paradisical truth to poems.

Yet, today, I fall like a blunt object into respites, walk forgetful among the wind-blown shrubs and brackish estuaries on this day of unplanned sun, happy to be lost in the world's things, in all this matter and *dura mater*, to feel when I speak, in each word, a sweet tensile pull of a string.

Afternoon light is penetrant, a blank, absented fixity. What birds have flown off I will find in glossaries; old loves I will find in the mind's book between a cloud and a branch or a filament of moon in the intense blue.

And perhaps I will stumble, as in a vision, on all the dead, mother and father included, lining the shore of Little Tick Island where they will be busy bowing to that figure of perfect freedom, their self-same minds.

And in the distance, like a memory of love's midpoint, I'll see the sun flash white on the salt-caked weather sides of twisted trees.

HETEROGLOSSIA ON FIFTY THIRD

Streets of a city, I walk and lose the hour.
Today, unsure of what I write, I circumambulate
the new and the ruin, find it
twelve noon amidst museums and gleaming limousines.
A bag lady shouts "I am entitled!" I also
am entitled to my thoughts at least, yet all day,
dream or nightmare do my talk, undo my walk,
so I let talk pitch self into doze or dream and chat:
man, woman, testicle, dessert. The language falls,
a chunk of disembodied sound through space.

My body sometimes feels like a corpse, but talk hears talk,
and I'm entitled in the streets, astride the century's
fatted calf, the pavement-glutted bowel. The talk of
street people is a groaning, each to each; I have heard
them singing on the trash. Ghost words, ghost fuckers!
They utter their words right out to do their ravaging
in me, joining my dead lords of speech like animals
granted province over those on whom they prey.

IN CENTRAL PARK

See, the bee emerges.
The furred dart sails
Across the grass, its whirr

Lost in the greater buzzing.
Like us, an after-trope
Is visible: hives, structures, cities.

Is the gatherer of nectar
A bourgeois or a communard?
Am I supposed to mind which?

Today, I read of one philosopher's
Impassioned hope. "Domestication,"
He writes, "is irreversible."

Above the trees, the high-risers
Float, perforce, before the sun.
In the streets, the comings and goings,
The endless traffic . . .

What dance there is
Must be saved for within
That honeyed fortress.

JURY DUTY IN MANHATTAN

That the law is blind, lovely and precise,
but that the blade rips air below the balance.

That the room reeks of municipal staleness, and so
thermostats are checked. That father-right and property

are base notes to legal melody. *Oh yeah, oh yeah*
is hummed by the young man called today.

And that the sound of killing time entombs the room:
the lawyer's drone like an artist's shoptalk

about the end of composition, the mural's tugboat
frozen midstream in paint between Liberty and the city.

ADULATION

for A.S.

"Adulation? Why, it's the structure of the world," said my friend. "Something more complex than mere appreciation."

As he spoke, he was studying the expression on my face, for there is nothing he enjoys more than to make a toy of my understanding.

"Listen," he went on, gearing up to provoke. "You've trained in the sciences. Imagine a statistical study of applause as it is heard these days at concerts or performances. Imagine measuring that pandemonium which contains everything from climactic relief to the feel of one's ticket money well spent. I may be wrong, but I notice a nearly obscene animation on the part of audiences no matter whether the event is any good or not. Dance, music, theater? Those sitting in the seats produce, as though under contract, oceanic tides of claps, howls, bravos! And the objects of such applause are required to stand, to bow, to bring themselves before the curtains, to front the mobs while severed from their performances and roles like butterflies forced back to being caterpillars and chrysallises. What truncations!"

"But," I returned, "you make it sound almost like some game, some ritual of formalized gestures: show ends, audience cheers, that sort of thing without regard for content."

My friend snarled: "A game? *Oh no!* In a game, two play, two get hot from the activity like two sticks rubbed on each other. There are sparks, fire, interchange! In today's auditorium we have a different system at work: one-way energy, parasitic leeching, pig-hunger, zip going to zap but no zap coming back. *In today's auditorium,*" he began to raise his voice but mastered himself, "the audience's psychic recesses are muddied up as by a stick, swirled in a swamp. It's out-and-out piggery: 'Oh dig into me, into my wild striated unimagined livings, etc. and etc...' the audience croons." He paused, then went on. "Adulation is *ex post facto* foreplay."

30

"What are you getting at?" I interjected.

My friend played at being lost in himself. "Those flushed faces," he sighed. "You know," he suddenly fixed on me, "I have had the fortune, good or bad, to be invited to numerous benefits, the kind where in the name of some worthy cause, rather well-off but otherwise undistinguished people gather in some public room with a sprinkling of celebrities, a famous conductor or playwright, for example. What occult occasions. At one side of a well-carpeted room are a gathering of nouveau riche anonymities, and there, across the velvety spaces, perhaps with the organizer of the function, is the renowned guest. These two sit on armchairs in semi-repose affecting intimacy while little by little the adulators leave their small knots of friends, these drab pigeons, and drag their long faces like broken wings or like glowing piglets to nuzzle at the guest. What abjectness must accompany this activity; no one can come away clean from such an encounter, even while it reverberates with its mystical dissonance. 'O dazzling reflector of my soul,' that long face mutters, 'O exemplar who breaks the mold and makes more human my ownership of seven supermarkets in Scarsdale.' The celebrity here, you see, is a kind of wondrous mirror, giving back the life before it *precisely* by containing all that is behind the mirror, all that would utterly flatten the pigeon standing before him. And so much the better if the pigeon, through some quirk of commercial awareness, should find in the haughty features of the famous, the flaws, the vast ennui or the facial tic by which the prince of the people may be brought down. Surely what is operant here is the fantastic love of one's own clay which turns every utterance of praise or understanding into a verbal backstroke!"

Now my friend, with this tirade, had made me a bit uneasy. I had only the other day been standing before the portals of Grand Central Station watching the well-dressed commuters piling through to catch their trains for the northern suburbs. I had thought then of the immense skies over suburbs, of their soft light, of autumn over their houses, that light in which trees seemed to dissolve and stars appear as

31

free miracles, of the crisp dry leaves on the ground. How delineated were the sky, the brick, the stone walls of houses with lamps at the windows, shelter, nest, the furrow of a known woman. What a miraculous thing it must be to return there after the theater with a vanquished feeling in one's chest. Adulation! Adulation! It seemed the nearest thing to death, I wanted to cry out, thinking of the sonorities, the textures of having touched the hem of greatness. The immaculate cleansing.

My face must have displayed my strange feelings.

"You know," my friend said, "it doesn't end there. No sooner have these people returned home from their gala, then the phones begin to buzz, 'Today I was at a cocktail party with you know who...', 'how wonderful, let me know when such a thing happens again.'"

My friend had a great smile on his face. "Then the network begins! Soon an entire world of pig messages, of this piglet love-talk is going on." He began to prance around the room, oinking and snorting, with dramatic sowlike turns. At first, I imagined he was doing this for my benefit, but no, he was losing himself in his little game.

Beautiful, beautiful, I thought and began clapping.

Whereupon he stopped, turned, glared at me and left the room.

Nevertheless I was sure he would call me the next day.

STROPHES FROM THE WRITINGS OF
WALTER BENJAMIN

In shutting out experience,
the eye perceives an experience
of a complementary nature,

less the product of facts
firmly anchored in memory

more a convergence in memory
of accumulated facts,

the replacement of older narrations
by information of sensation.

According to theory,
fright's significance
in the absence
of ready anxiety.

FOR PAUL BLACKBURN

Living between the boulders
Of the world

That grind down
The boulder of the self

There falls the fine powder
That comes of grinding
So soft it is to touch

False softness

Roll this rock back
From the damp ground
Through which water seeps
—the rock become
As frangible
As earth—

And the worm bores entrance
Before its time

MONTAIGNE

This bundle of so many disparate pieces
is being composed in this manner:
I set my hand to it only
when pressed by too unnerving an idleness,
and nowhere but at home.

I want to represent the course
of my humours; I want people
to see each part at its birth.

I have grown seven or eight years
older since I began, not
without some new acquisition.

Through the liberality of the years
I have become acquainted
with the kidney stone.

It was, precisely, of all the accidents
of old age, the one I feared most.
For my soul takes no other alarm

but that which comes
from the senses
and the body. I have at least

this profit from the stone:
that it will complete what I have
still not been able to accomplish,

to reconcile and familiarize myself
completely with death.

The more my illness oppresses me
the less will death be something
to fear.

God grant that in the end, if its sharpness
comes to surpass my powers, it may not
throw me back to the other extreme, no less
a vice, of loving and desiring death....

I have always considered that precept
formalistic which so rigorously and precisely
orders us to maintain a good countenance
in the endurance of pain.

What matter if we twist our arms,
provided we do not twist our thoughts.
Philosophy trains us for ourselves,
not for others; for being, not seeming.

It is cruelty to require of us
so composed a bearing. Let this care
be left to the actors and teachers of rhetoric.

If there is relief in complaining,
let it be so. If we feel pain evaporates
somewhat for crying out,

or that our torment is distracted,
let us shout right away. If we play
a good game, it is a small matter
that we make a bad face.

IN THE SCHOOL

Open window has a grille.

Air going by assails.

Sky's blue, piercing through,
is gloom. Teacher's defensive tone,
textbook poems he admires: celebrations
of the West, Frostian walks in woods.
"I write a few myself," he tells me
"when emotions hit....my father's death,
the day my nine-year-old said 'Don't
touch or kiss me' . . . ," pauses, looks
towards shelf. Light falls
on close-packed spines of books.

Screams and shouts behind us
in halls and yards
and voices raised
to an inevitable almost sexual hate
because the air which fills the room
is not the window's air
which in its passage seems like the words of an art,
roiling desire with its touch.
Our lives are out of reach.

What air remains
is high in the children's throats.

SESTINA: OFF SEASON

These are the poets' times, these dark times,
for the world takes as real its own fanatic thought.
A realibus ad realiora, the words build a hexagram
of stagnant heavens while peasants do their work and fall,
the superior ones do their managing and seek reclusion
in their summerings beside the sunblasted light of the sea.

The poet would rather borrow from the moon-puddled sea,
but how give up the coiled worm gnawing at the times,
burn up the page, put the word in reclusion
until only the sandy coasts are objects of a thought
and history can be thrown for a ten-count fall
— the cry of nothing — of ghost birds, cage, a hexagram

for poets who hexagram
their luxuries beside the sea,
who swoon and fall,
whose visions are multiples of love times
lovers, endless self-circles of thought
in secret fondness of their reclusion.

O poet, car roofs and glass glint under leafy reclusion
and one must give heart to vocabularies of the hexagram.
One must be at pains to see the world glitter in mere thought,
to see the cruelty in the lives of animals and in the high sea
of our leaders' rhetoric which downs the very times
and makes of these last grace notes a mechanic fall.

Compose; if necessary, compose against the fall.
For god's sake, leave this elysian reclusion!
Note how sea-scud and bird-lime mark the times,
how the lines flatten to this one sad hexagram
of hope, the moon's pearl puckering a violent sea
as poetry despairs of any cogent thought.

That poet who warned of unsightly sifting sands of thought
entered into the very end of time's articulated fall
where every word is borne upon a flood as if heaven's sea

were an earth of inundated lands. Uncover! Mind performs
    reclusion
as though recounted lives were pent beneath a hexagram
of yarrow stalks, spelling, in emboldened crumblings, our
    times.

Too long is the word disembodied from our pain while
    reclusion
buffers body. Unbuild this great vast hexagram
whose rigid lines make misprisons of poets from loves' times.

III

OUTSIDE A CLASSROOM IN NERJA

"Ayer, cinco pescadores morir"

Grey clouds massed
over waves and horizons.
Light bands itself to peaks
and to the sea, an enormous
tarnished plate their boats must plow.
Existence, a constant birth of signs
rising toward this, their outward life,
febrile, thinner than air, idea
no more than a glimmer unless a word
slams home its bolt.

In the narrow streets,
walls painted with flaking lime,
where at night, children sit
in front of firepots and see,
in the maze of lines, clowns
or dancing bears — faces carried
to bed with delicious frights.
The ever-readable randomness.

In the morning, to stand beside
the school, peer through the window glass.
No inklings of the lessons. Only
to watch the teacher talk, the teacher
who has the eyes of her poor dumb
fisherman father, eyes which look
at the children as he looked daily at the sea,
the same small anticipations and terrors.
      Perhaps her words catch the waves'
dead glint, but explain indifference
or recalcitrance to a child?
      And now the small gyrations
of her hands, as she tells something
to the children — whatever is being
said — are as beautiful
as the wind-shaped clouds
above the mountains.

43

TOURIST'S CAVE

I.

Stood on the floor of stone
The names given to the many chambers:
Hall of the Cataclysm
Hall of the Cascade
Hall of the Phantoms

Stood on the floor
And the lights, the lamps of red, green, yellow
On the stone flutings and the water-worn

And the man who rediscovered the cave,
When the boys brought him to the entrance
— it had gone unnoticed all those years —
He flashed his beam down the pit's mouth
"and the light fell," he said,
"so that nothing stopped it.
It went on and on to hell itself," he said.

But hell was not there,
Was above in the air
Where one walks.

II.

Like the odor of wild thyme
Found on the hillside clinging to the hands,
The sense of this place clings to the eye.

Air so clear
It sings the white of painted houses.

Beneath the eaves of the Alcalde's house,
Abandoned nests of the African stork.
Like the tourist, an erratic synapse
Brings them flocking to the town
Every four or five years going north.

And the rich and the poor alike live locked in a profusion
Of flowers; no spring, no season, but the geranium,
The bougainvillaea are always there, and the not-so-rich
And the newly rich tend also
The plastic flower.

Tourist's eye of seamless pastoral.

But at night, firepots wink before hovels, lights,
Lights of houses on the hill.

"O look into the eyes,
O begin with the eyes,
eyes wide
In the dark."

III.
At Lario's estate,
An iron gate is mortared to a wall
At the end of the village's poorest street.
Through bars, a garden is disclosed
Where one of every flower grows, and footpaths
Lined with polished planter's wood
Steal all the flyblown eyes.

Please – or not so politely – the villagers
Are forcibly removed.
Pitiless sun is given to this un-mask:
Not scarcity
But greed in a plenitude of light.

Removal from sunlight
Is the history of their kind.

IV.
Firepots wink before the hovels,
Lights of houses on the hill.

Where they are gathered, they talk
About the fearful night.

For it is night in the world now,
And the dark does nothing

But remind them of their own dark.

V.
One night we came down from the mountain village by the
route which followed the dry river bed, a vast expanse of white
boulders, pale and dusty in the moonlight. We had come this
way before only in daylight, and were now being guided along
by one of the townspeople returning home. As we came to that
part of the riverbed nearly a quarter-mile wide, I could see lights
flickering high on the walls of the cliffs which marked the old
banks of the river. What are those lights, I asked? *Animales,*
replied our guide. *Animales? Gitanoes,* he spat out. For here lived
the gypsies whom I had seen in town, dirty, ragged, the
children bitten by fleas and covered with sores. It was widely
believed the gypsies had the power to hex or curse, and many of
the disturbances such as bad weather, bad fishing or ruined har-
vests were blamed on them. None of the gypsies lived in town.
No one would have had them, even if they could afford the
rents. I had wondered where they lived, and now I knew, the
caves, really great open holes in the cliff face. After dark, as one
walked this riverbed, it was their candles and lanterns which
one saw. And now, as we passed closer, led by our guide, we
could see these lights casting curious shadows on the walls, out-
lining the massive rims of rock which sheltered them, so that it
looked to us as if they were living inside an enormous human
skull.

VI.
This to say of the neural chains
On which thoughts ride.
They too are completely in the dark,
Like creatures of a cave,
Blinder than moles that tunnel.

VII.
"Living nights," we called them.
That whistle in high woods above the riverbed
Which followed us for miles.
One could hear it above the stream's trickle,
Above the sounds of our breath bouncing back
From the narrowing gorge's walls, hear it
Until the rocks seemed about to seize us,
The two cliffs face to face
The way no one could be with any of them
And not draw up his own terror
Cold and quick as the torrent of water
Swirling about our feet
Which we tried to shout above
For some nameless quality of contact.

VIII.
The chambers named
The colored bulbs which play

To hell had the light gone
And in the strata, the clay pot and the bone,
The great white bone exposed in the strata

And the lamps red, green and yellow,
And for the first time, heard there,
With the others, drowning voice and time,
The piped-in music

And the drawings of the ram and of the bull
Were for years undiscovered
— such pains to do their work in secret

And the named chambers which led to "hell itself"
—the floors of which,
The bones and the axe in the strata

And the eyeless fish
Can know nothing of the light
Know nothing
Of the red, the green nor of the yellow

STATUE: JARDIN DU LUXEMBORG

The grass tips rise, pale white field daisies
grow in clumps, green surrounded by sandy gravel,
paths, benches, statuary, students having their lunch
in the bright sun, oo la la all this in French.

The grass reads out the Father's epoch, obscure
and bound in creation's knot, and the epoch of the Son
squats in the greensward, in curved bronze
captured in upthrust: *Les Etudiants de la Resistance.*
No comfort in the patina's uncanny cold, in
the hollow structure of the Patriarch's leg
to which the youthful figures cling.

Our epoch is to live with these two,
Father and Son in time, to repeat endlessly
these cycles of grass and bronze. Yet Paris encircles
like our Mother, incrustations of plaster on plaster,
centuries of wear, humans stuccoed to the pile,
these little affections to outweigh a dream of monuments...

The city stretches off into sun-watered light.
To be in love with this minute is to be
in love with air displaced by metal.

ON A LINE FROM BAUDELAIRE

at Père Lachaise

"The dead, the poor dead, have their bad hours"
If there are the dead, have they lived in vain?
Things continue, it all says, the stars bulge and quiver,
The neutrino beats, the oxidizing of metals
Heats modernity. In Paris, over the poor dead,
The tombstones fascinate, the cats hide in
Marble and shrubbery, the walls are like a vise
And enclose. Once they asked for flowers, too late,
For flowers. Green spring honors the living but who
Begged? The spring resonates with her silk; even gravel
Sings, the worm has turned me to poetry. The dead,
The powdered rich: names are taken. History spirals
Into the center of this conch shell, the air swirls
Over Paris, out of reach, lives on, dies on.
The airs of the universe beat oceanic
On these well set up stones.

CLIMB TO AN ANCIENT CHATEAU IN FRANCE

at Lastours

Stones spilled out of ruins
arouse an ardor in me. So hard
to climb there I confuse

standing on the precipice with
some out-of-the-century height, some
out-of-the-body jest by which to take

in the eye's sweep and laugh, at our feet
all bloody Europe. Effects of clear air
only faintly tinged with rank perfume of shrubs,

of nibbling goats. We pick our way, animal-like,
among rocks, not for bittersweet verdure but to believe
for a moment the escape from time's laminate,

the hawk made cognate with the boom
and the contrail. And then,
that brilliant zephyr of fear, to lose
the ground rock, the affection for

the elemental. And yet, with another to share,
to be here, hand in hand, thus, what to ask?
In asperous loveliness, catch breath, lie

as one in high grass, our bodies rapt
in what is present, mind vacant
as the calendar's unused blank.

The saxifrage clings, and the pattern is broken.
And possibly a word can survive like this:
a stone parted from its mortar, the discourse
of contours, striations and lichen.

FIFTY THREE RUE NOTRE DAME DE NAZARETH

"Paris
Paris
Of your beautiful phrases"

I.
Isn't this the window?
And this the *troisieme étage?*
Just another dream above that zero base,
The hardened sites of syntax,
From which the populace's many tongues
Rise into their pain,
No two minds, nor worlds, alike.

Apartment borrowed, I have also borrowed
This language, another's plangent, torn bon mot,
This world, *l'écriture*, a borrowing,
And I've looked below, cut from the cloud burst
Mottled sky to see the borrowed ones of France,
These North Africans who gamble in the street.

I've been absorbed in examinations:
There, the very top of an ear,
The sculpted ebony's shiny flue.
Also, I've watched the games they play
On crate tops chalked with numbered squares,
Playgrounds of this *la malbolgia lumière.*

I have seen this from above,
For I am of the imperious gaze, the leaseholder
Of the view, and cannot help but note
These gaming wooly heads,

Cannot help but hear their click speech,
Their lover-words, their shouts, and all these
Bespeak my vantage, my political,
My pâté-laden table. Oh I have looked,

And I have seen! Disembodied tropes
Of the century's textual warpings.

II.

As another legatee of Mallarmé,

I have strained against the tongue
Until the word displaced
The world's foreign body,

Have played with the exclusionary pun,
And yet, and yet,

Have sat and let my life go
Into this beautiful table laid with foods:
Cheeses, wines, *légumes en vinaigrette,*
Let eye catch the tin patina-ed roofs,
The balcony's potted plant, saw across
The way through gauze, a woman
In her underclothes ironing a blouse
Beneath a blazing chandelier,
In broad daylight.

And I have wondered if
The poem need witness,
Or simply come to take its place
Beside such lovely things.

O how generous to rest
Without predator's intent
Among one's other possessions.

III.

At night, dressed in white, in at least
Three rented rooms that I can see,

Arab shopworkers face east and are supine.
In white and supine, in the murderous arcs
Of nearly flattened bodies,

They face east and are supine,
jihad scrawled on wall against…

And this mecca is a rock,
Its hammer: a bone
Lodged in flesh.

IV.
During the day, they listen to
The cardboard carton's amplifying sounds.
One man is decorous, another's smile is sweet,
An urban gazelle's or desert creature's grace
As he shakes the dice-man's hand,
And the pleasantries are not French
Nor ritual, nor colonial jujubes,

Rather, cosmos is invoked
In the *brinng, brinng, brinng,*
Dice rattling in the cup.

V.
Brinnng, brinng

So much of the noise
One has no part in:
Machines which hum in shops
Or the foreman's edgy drone
That make for a ghetto slum of sounds

Against which the rattled dice
Sound a kind of *no one means this;*
They lie there being nothing but themselves.

While at best one writes
The lightning's thunderclap:
Not the event itself, but the event's
Near after. Poet, this is the husk

Already burnt, the belated desiring
Of an image on command,
O not one's own, never one's own.

VI. *Collage:*
"impossible not to be gripped by the spectacle of this
sickly population which swallows the dust of factories,
breathes in particles of cotton and lets its tissues be permeated
by white lead, mercury and all the poisons
needed for the production of masterpieces... of this
languishing and pining population to *whom the earth owes its
wonders.*"

"Again I lean on the rough granite of the embankment
As if I had returned from travels through the underworlds"

We have come by myriad gates:
The arch at the top of Saint-Martin,
Portals, canals, boulevards,
Borders to be traversed,
Lines of poplars shimmering in summer heat.

Look down rows of statuary and buildings,
The famous tower drawing down the sky,
A brilliant landscape of gods, beasts, men
Who wander in that seamless envelope of mind.

And there are grimy courts, alleyways,
Masoned cul-de-sacs, lightless baffles,
Shut-outs.

From travels, returning to the underworlds,
To find every word another brick in these brick walls.

VII.
Chase a number until it's marked
A counterpoint of nought

Chase a number and fall supine.
All set things come down in the null
Against which history has built
Its concrete, its blood-stained showings

The dice reverberate with a call
To a cosmos set apart, gamblers
Conjoined to the noise-making myth:

universe, chaste and free,
made of these called up sounds
the hasard *inverts the real*
no longer telling hope but truth

IV

SOME ANTHROPOLOGY

And yet poems remind me of the tribe of the gentle Tasaday
who some regard merely as members of another tribe taught
to fool anthropologists with false primitiveness and naïveté,
to be blunt in their manners and infernally innocent. No one
is sure, as with poems, whether they are real or a hoax,
whether the dictator, in his munificence, created a forest
preserve to shelter them as he might set aside an apartment
for a poet in the palace. Forests and palaces, such utopias are
mostly exclusionary, like hotels for the rich, and needn't
concern us. It is rainy for a rain forest to house our myths, to
shelter our lost tribes, who, one by one, gather in a clearing.
I sometimes think about my lost tribe of Jews, American
Jews, also part hoax and part invention, whose preserve is
sheltered under brick where limousines hum and one hears
the faint, familiar babble of the homeless. As it happens, the
Tasaday are being declared "nonexistent" by government
scientists so their hardwood forests can be transformed into
chests of drawers. Strange, then, the anthropology of the
poet who must build his poems out of the myths he intends
to falsify, who says, look my friend, you are laying away
your laundered shirts in a rain forest.

THE AMERICAN JEWISH CLOCK

When did Solomon (for Zalman) Heller, my grand-
father, come here, his time folded into America
like honey layered in middle-European pastry?

When did he arrive? After his pogroms and wars,
And before my father's. Was he naive? To arrive
like an autocrat, to enter like a king, in the train

of minor victories. Zalman, here called Solomon!
With a new syllable to lengthen his name. In the vast
benumbed space of us, a little more sound to place him.

Were there sour Jewish chives on his tongue,
Yiddish chimes in the bell of his breath?
He knew very little English, but he cocked his ear.

He heard the clock sounds that translate every-
where. He had been brought into redeeming time,
each stroke the echo of his unappearing God.

With tick came the happy interregnum,
those Twenties and Thirties when profit
turned to loss, and loss to profit.

Tock came later when the synagogues swelled
with increase and were tethered like calves
on suburban lawns. And then . . . . O and then,

the young walked out, walked back
to the cities, prodigals of emptied memory.
I was among them. And the door slammed shut.

And the space outside, that endlessness to America,
was ululated on every word but tick and tock.

IN A DARK TIME, ON HIS GRANDFATHER

Zalman Heller, writer and teacher, d. 1956

There's little sense of your life
Left now. In Cracow and Bialystok, no carcass
To rise, to become a golem. In the ground

The matted hair of the dead is a mockery
Of the living root. Everyone who faces
Jerusalem is turned back, turned back.

It was not a question of happiness
Nor that the Laws failed, only
That the holy or sad remains within.

This which cleft you in the possibility
Of seeing Him, an old man
Like yourself.

Your last years, wandering
Bewildered in the streets, fouling
Your pants, a name tag in your coat

By which they led you back,
Kept leading you back. My father
Never spoke of your death,

The seed of his death, as his death
To come became the seed, etc . . . . Grandfather,
What to say to you who cannot hear?

The just man and the righteous way
Wither in the ground. No issue,
No issue answers back this earth.

FOR UNCLE NAT

I'm walking down 20th Street with a friend
When a man beckons to me from the doorway
Of Congregation Zichron Moshe. "May I,"
He says to my companion, "borrow this
Jewish gentleman for a moment?" I follow
The man inside, down the carpeted aisle,
Where at the front, resplendent in
Polished wood and gold, stands
The as yet unopened Ark.

Now the doors slide back, an unfolded
Promissory note, and for a moment,
I stand as one among the necessary ten.
The braided cloth, the silver mounted
On the scrolls, even the green of the palm
Fronds placed about the room, such hope
Which breaks against my unbeliever's life.

So I ask, Nat, may I borrow you, for a moment,
To make a necessary two? Last time we lunched,
Enclaved in a deli, in the dim light, I saw
A bit of my father's face in yours. Not to make
Too much of it, but I know history
Stamps and restamps the Jew; our ways
Are rife with only momentary deliverance.
May I borrow you for a moment, Nat. We'll celebrate
By twos, the world's an Ark. We'll talk in slant,
American accent to code the hidden language of the Word.

ACCIDENTAL MEETING WITH AN ISRAELI POET

At the playground by the Con Ed plant,
this is strange: from tall brick stacks,
smoke is bleeding off into cloudless sky.
Little dreams, little visions must go like that.

Still, his boy and mine play in their soccer game,
each move, each kick or run precise and self-
contained. From one end of the field to the other

they go, from sun to deep shade. And there's no
poof, no gone, no fade into that all-capping blue.
Trampled ground, grass, sun-tinged webs of cable—

so this is how we reckon hope, as something
blotted up by matter that it might better
circulate in brick, in the squared-off shadows

of the powerplant to commingle with children
and with games and sides, with wire and with steel
until, lo, the helmet of a soldier has sopped it up!
It sits there, insisting on a certain rightness.

And yet people's songs disperse into the air,
people's songs and rhetoric . . .

PALESTINE

I.
Snow glides down in the west Forties.
Like a child, I could lick the snowflakes
from my wrists. In storms,
bums will nibble at the wood of tenement doorways.
The weather precipates dreams, fantasies, I too
have my dreams of the snow's purity,
of its perfecting worlds, so little like my own.
Could I be a gentleman of this snow, my calling card
one evanescent flake to place upon a blemish?

Frankly, I'm delighted with a new scientific proof:
at any moment at least two places on the globe
must experience similar weather. Hence my
Palestine and hence my joy. Baudelaire
watched the Negress in the street stomp her feet
and imagine date palms. I don't want the territory,
just the intensity of a visit. Sh'ma Yisrael, only
the symbol world holds you and me or I and Thou.
Sh'ma Palestine, aren't you always where snow falls.

II.
My Palestine, which means I love one woman,
so why not two? Which means I love that distant sky
and the lovely irritants of my inner eye. My tears
for what in life is missed. The Red Sea of my philosophy
will irrigate with salt these barren lands.

Does snow fall there too?

III.
Always somewhere else, and always held by someone else…
Sweet figs, sweet thighs to Suez or Port Said.
But when snow falls one's place is yet another place.

IV.

In that salty biblical sweetness, why avenge?
Grief is vectored north, east, west, the Wailing Wall.
Why avenge? Terror has cast its rigid mask,
and with fraternal semblance, transformed all
into sisters and brothers. Why avenge?
Only the dead wear human faces.

V.

Yea, though I am not lifted out of sorrow,
yea, though the opus of self-regard endoweth me
for nearly nothing, I have not forgotten snow. I
have no more forgotten snow than other poets forget
time or blackbirds. I have, with love, put the snow aside,
I have let the snow melt so that I may envision Judea
as a stately gentile lady, a crusader, a crusade.

VI.

I am so far away,
yet for Americans
distances are musical.
So I am near. I am with snow
which softens the city in which I live.
I am in the Forties and the snow glides down
and fills all the niches that lie between
the living and the dead.

MAMALOSHON

At night, dream sentences
That will not write themselves.

And there are phrases
You forget. Dawn comes;

It's only luck
Her breast is not your mother's.

So much touched by words,
At least you live.

What escapes makes for the grave—
A respectable marker.

CONSTELLATIONS OF WAKING

on the suicide of Walter Benjamin
at the Franco-Spanish border, 1940

Something you wrote:
"Eternity is far more
the rustle of a dress

than an idea."
What odd sounds
to listen to

beneath occluded skies
that darken rivers,
Dnieper, Havel, Ebro,

murmuring contained
between
their tree-lined banks...

"In the fields
with which we are concerned,

knowledge comes only
in flashes. The text
is thunder rolling

long afterwards."
And thus, and thus...

   *

These constellations,
which are not composed of stars
but the curls of shrivelled leaves

by which the tree expressed
the notion of the storm. You
lived in storm, your outer life:

"adversities on all sides
which sometimes came
as wolves." Your father—

Europe was your father
who cast you on the path,
hungry, into constellated cities:

Berlin, Moscow, Paris.
Where would
Minerva's owl alight,

on what dark branch
to display its polished
talons?

*

1940
and in Paris, the library
is lost.

Books
no longer on the shelves —
how sweetly

they were "touched," you wrote
"by the mild boredom
of order."

*

Curled leaf,
one among many
on trees that lead

to a border crossing.
But black wolves in France,
they have changed the idea

of eternity. Toward
Port Bou, bright dust
mixing

with the ocean's salt air.
Wave-fleck from train:
each spun light

must have its meaning.
So to consider
as ultimate work

that sea bed of
all citation—
you'd allow nothing of your own—

thus the perfected volume.
No author?
And then no death?

The sea is inscribed
with *The Prayer*
for the Dead. No

author and then
no death? But the leaf
acquired shadow by

the ideal of light,
scattered light
the father

never recognizes.
The books are not
on shelves,

for that was Paris.
This the closed road
from Port Bou

which glistens with the dew
of morning. Redemptive
time

which crystallizes
as tree, as leaf
on the way to a border.

V

TWO SWANS IN A MEADOW
BY THE SEA

High dunes falling away
To spongy ground, water lying
In brackish shallow pools
A few feet from the surf.

Broom and high grass hide
A dozen birds. They twitter.
We take it in as best we can,
The sea's sound, all
The marvelous growth.

No need to ask, to answer
How sky and hilly tufts,
Noise of cars on the road above

Are so composed to bring us,
Our eyes level with the sea,
To where two white forms
Rest their lovely necks
As though in self-caress,
Looking at each other.

A NIGHT FOR CHINESE POETS

at Newcastle, Wyoming

All day, to have met with poets,
Bureaucrats, teachers, to be weary
Of one's own kind, of the numberless

Diamonds and snowflakes written in
Children's poems. Then at the motel
Where the running fountain builds an immense

Sea anemone of glittering ice—the ducks
That forgot to go south quack around it—
I sit down to write you a letter, perhaps

A poem. And outside the moon turns the North Platte
Into frozen jade. Remember Li Shang-yin's jade
Pieced into a screen behind which she moved,

His love, his lucid madness. Now Orion's points
Are clear. The heavens bind at his girdle.
Wind glazes the puddles in the road,

Carries toward me the snow owl's shriek,
Thought and distance making hellish antipodes.
What now of the ink-laden brush which "once

Forced the elements?" Weather beats at the window
Above the desk. I think of other Northern wastes,
A small boat tethered in an icy stream,

The exiled poet poised, regarding the paper's
Snowy white, "brooding on the uselessness
Of letters." *World, world,* invisible escort,

Messenger of the conjure-god, my bed's sweet
Ghost. I want to cry like one possessed
That this emptiness bears a shred-end of you
Into the room, that the heart is no less
For the page alone.

JANUARY NIGHTS

Sitting alone in a warm room.
Colors of brown, cream, gold.

My privacy extends to walls. I want
To exclaim that I am safe. Safe from what?

Beyond this is air, universe...
The lungs burn and the stars burn

With a suggested correspondence.
To imagine that I am just a nuance

Of what is happening, a trace
On the mandala of a poetry made

Out of the uncertain ache for certainty.
The paper's whiteness medicinally cool.

*

Light falls. Clouds pile as scud
Under the moon. In the west

A diffuse glow. Stopped traffic
And stars to be seen.

Only the lump ebony
Of the telephone

Outshines the night.
The moon looks iron.

Sister of cycles,
It pulls earth and tide,

Wave-tips of matter
Caught in repetitions.

Nearly mad with loneliness,
I rise, go to the window like many another.

*

The lights blaze in the great structures.
The air between, with swirls of snow, glows red.

Street, gutter, show tracks of a lone straggler.
Marks the wind will blow away.

But the sky is unstaunched, unswabbed
Of its endlessness: an angry blossom of love.

*

By the playground, the sky looks caged.
Moon shines amid patchy squares.

The swing creaks and the iron bars
Make a geometry.

Thoughts crowd of wanted toys.
Now, nothing as simple as that happiness

Nor the easy discard of broken things.
Pain is sharp — the space between us

Revealing realm upon realm
Of assailing glamour.

A WEEKEND OF SUN

I.
What did I want to say? The building edge cut
bright blue air. Up Madison, a kind of favoring

light. Gauds of the world were there, glistening
gobs of silver swirled in tailored shrouds,

then doubled in backlit mirrors which gave us
back ourselves. We'd risen from sleep's

charnel ground to see our figures in the glass
beside the bracelet on its velvet pad, alone in *luxe.*

We laughed. I looked at your high cheekbones,
half-buttoned blouse, dark studied contours.

I was the student of this theater, yet how to act my part?
Mind a cooled flame. Anticipation, the great, the absurd
        mentor.

The sun's corolla flared pride and sex;
the street's air was all magnetic storm.

II.
Downtown then, we joined the Soho crowds
in that odd net, the modern become medieval,

in throngs to which we all belonged. Grime
in pavement cracks, tattered posters

of the week's events, I wandered out, a tourist
of identities. I watched a man on high stilts

who played the people's grand buffoon. More laughter.
Story was dead, we agreed. Here was sun, obliterating

memory while we, like mathematicians, summed analogs
with gesture and with dress. Sat too and chatted.

Irony, giddy irony, an empyrean of corrosive talk
as further away, on tall slabs of downtown stone,

sun fired glass. Up, up, the light burned
climbing that building, seeking for the roof

where one could open the firedoor at the top
and illumine the building's hollows.

Laughter which transmutes. In bar light,
mascara streaked. A face shocked into pain. Done.

III.
Then through streets to the Square;
in the sunlight, each self an auto-de-fé

to burn on the regard of others —
bars and cafes our rehearsal halls,

our as yet unplayed dramas. More talk, dazzling
and accusatory, also brought more clarity.

Beside us, things we drank and ate: wine, cheese,
ashes smudged on cloth. We had added to the paraphernalia,

would make of common props an aesthetic
of the empirical, and we would see.

IV.
That afternoon, to make love, to try to throw away
signpost, route, city map, direction, to enter

some unknowable. The light came as through a curtain
on a stage. That sun in the window exposed between us

an increment of space, a last blurred fortress of our holding.
We spoke of what was false but wanted true: ways of knowing

to become ways of celebration. We had become two words, two
parts stripped of meaning, sounding for each other only an
echo.

LATE VISIT

And wasn't it the traffic of the world
we heard five flights up?
If it was street noise,
it was also more. The windows rattled,
our arms and legs rocked backward,
thrashed out a scripted pain-blocking lust.
Your words came fast, like the buzz
of an engraving on a shiny bone or tusk.

At the window,
where curtains blocked
a human-reminding light,
muffled wheel and shout,
the unheard, you said,
was a shroud. It played
itself amidst the dishes,
wire and antenna to the clouds
which moved so slowly past,
so slowly past,
as though the sky
had grown external skin:
an anti-music to the music of all things.

Only a recluse
could hear it, you said.
Unuttered it came with the light
between the cooing plaints:
"I too sought another, sought another . . . "

BEING AT EAST HAMPTON

I.
"The Hamptons are the playground of the artists."

From within the yard of the little house
I like to paint, on Fabriano or D'Arches,
Cars pulled in under low trees.

At one time I used a child's set of paints;
Now I squib the tube's bright colors
Onto a palette made of plastic.

This preparation looks forbidding,
Even contemporary – the hand holding
The brush an already anxious object.

Miles from the city, the ancient subjects
Seem gifted and returned: sun, light,
Shrub, the shadow's play on the car's

Metallic sheen. Inapt machinery
Which cannot stand against an age.
Not modern in execution, my little

Pictures long for the hard surety
Of the classic. But my being here
Observing is both accident and intention

Blurring together like cars and trees,
Like any number of different natures
In the pigments and the washes.

II.
Perhaps you wouldn't like this place
With its petite talk of art,
Its dishonored hopes of wildness.

Here the gesture fails,
Is like the sky's immense expanse,
Something outside ourselves,
Irrelevant and almost comic.

As it turns out, this
Was no place to vaunt an independence.
Nothing here can stand alone,
Neither hope nor fear

Nor the isolate houses
On their spits of sand
In which the sea is heard

Reminding the occupants
That they are human.

III.
In the sun's glare, one scans
The bayside's waters. The blue above
Is lucid, pieced around the clouds,

Trees and houses in precise detail.
Where we take our dips,
A sheer boring fix of things

Even to the little knots
Of healthy-looking middle-class families.
This freeze-frame of an illusion

Now a broken-open social code
(good for all but the realist novelist).
Little one knows one's self,

One's time. Thus that scare of
Faint strangeness one late afternoon
When the fog rolled in upon our picnic;

On the island opposite,
Two mute swans we could have dreamed
Beat about each other
Like mad Japanese ghosts.

IV.
Bleep, bleep emits the antenna,
Beacon light across the bay.

Nights, the wind drops.
In the stillness, the mind

Suddenly a partisan of things.
To want to grip, to cleave to an image,
Read it as some self-secret text.

Meanwhile she moves into waves,
Sound of human noise enfolded
In the seas, in the watery zones.

A half-clear lightness
Extends to her body's depth,
Liquidity shading into dark.

Phantom of infiltration,
To whom or to what would you speak?

And the clouds gone as from the world,
The moon a mirror choked on dust.

V.
Again, the foam-tip dark of waves
Brings in on its curves
Images of living and of dying.

Not identity, but a visionary lesson
In the drama of the littoral.
And the birds come and go,
Are duly noted. I swear
We do not live on fixities,
Shells or stars which once discovered

Seem always with us. Do you remember,
These too, found amid
Those inland mountain tops?

Yet the sea…the sea does not strive
To emulate the granite.
You are here; no need to put this note

In a bottle in the breakers.
The sea is just…the sea a few feet away.
To give it that.

VI.
Today at the jetty, the wind
Lifts mother-of-pearl flakes
Off the beach.

One with a deep pink hue
Blows into a groove of stone.
In the pale light

It gleams: a gem set
In a cold setting. No sails
Cut the grey bay's foil.

The bird-lime dribbles hard
On the ledges of the rock.
A tossed-up shell

Pierced by a gull's beak
Shrills curiously in the wind.
Another held in the hand

Repeats the ocean mutedly.
Apart, apart, yet to make of this
A blended music.

The tidal pools respiring
As the ocean rejoins itself.

THIS MANY-COLORED BRUSH WHICH
ONCE FORCED THE ELEMENTS

to J.A. (– among Chinese paintings
of eight dynasties)

I.
Under an open window, palace ladies
tune the eight-stringed lute,
the one I love gone off to visit
a solitary temple amid clearing peaks.

She travels where the religious ones go,
following in their train, the peevish monks,
the fishermen, desiring to be devout,
the old with their trembling toes on Nirvana's gate,

who plod dutifully into winterstruck mountains,
to see the blossoming peonies of the snow
delicate as the ladies of the court.

Here I sit, with other dazed creatures
not knowing how to seek, too dumb to go south.
They must nestle in this leafless grove,
for the mountainous winter landscape
contains at least one bird
flitting from tree to peak to stream,
all the while singing for some knickknack peddler
who's made his fist of silver at the court.

When the seasons wheel through the year again,
perhaps my turn will come.

II.
Last year, two love-struck kids,
we gawked under the red cliff,
gazed in wonder at anchored boats.

I could smell the whiff of buffalo and calf
a child had driven to be bathed.
"Samantabhadra" he was muttering
as if the inland sea were some
Lotus Sutra-covered altar.

Contemplate what an arhat
and his attendants might do,
traveling among streams and mountains,
listening to a bird on a tree serenade a cataract.

Soon, when you return, we will go
to compose poetry on a spring outing.
Possibly, you will make verse and paint
the twelve views of the landscape,
the full sail on the misty river.
(Last time you let me put in
the five dragons, the two thin lines
that render Shakyamuni coming down the mountains.)

III.
When teachers are asked, we are told:
attend the water-and-moon Kuan-yin.
Bless deeply this place
for the river village is the fisherman's joy.
It flows from his full heart
into the sky like inked bamboo or a prunus
in the hidden moon's pale light.

Here, the nine horses and the nine songs
are as venerated as the treasured aspects
of the white-robed Kuan-yin. Here the Buddha
converts the *bhikshus.*

Honor also the bamboo, the rock and the tall tree.
There is both devotion and leisure enough to spare.
"Merits are like having a hundred birds and three friends."
So say the nine elders of the mountain of fragrance.

IV.
This haven of the peach-blossom spring
reminds me of the river village in a rainstorm.
Squirrels cavort among the grapes as in
a landscape in the style of Ni Tsan.

You remember his album: the five leaves
of Shen Chou. Also, the one leaf
that looks like three of Wen Cheng's.

V.
Much to understand.
I cannot give up my need for understanding.
So gladness to the scholar who returns
with his crane in the boat,
says his farewell to the unknowable Sea
of the North at Hsun-yang.

Such farewells blend like notes
of the many-stringed *ch'in* in a secluded valley.
Old cypress and rock in the jade field,
Emblematic of the mountains of Ch'ing Pien
which were as beautiful as the paintings
of the ancient masters:
cloudy peaks, landscape studies, companions
strolling, as we have done, in autumn hills.

The masters slyly ask, do you know the difference
between those mynah birds, old tree and rocks
and these mynah birds and rocks?

I will look for spring on the Min River
or in the shade of pines in a cloudy valley.

VI.

Chrysanthemums float in ink!
The tall bamboo is posed with distant mountains

as though in a landscape
— in the color style of Ni Tsan!
— as in a portrait of An Ch'i!

The leaves fall,
but the titles of paintings remain.
I have lived long enough to know
that I am in love with figments,
thigh-turns and orchid boats peeping shyly.

One thing I have learned from the sage:
"you cannot grasp even a moment."
But I at least remember
the titles of the paintings.

Words, leaves, the thick black turn of the brush.
I have thought of you while writing this,
of a conversation in storied autumn.

Yes, Han-shan and Shih-te are with us.
Voices as from a landscape with a waterfall.

WATER, HEADS, HAMPTONS

"the unbearableness of idyllic literature"
— C A N E T T I

My dear,
it is summer. Time to be out of time.
Let us read together the world's newspapers.

But the wind blows away the pages of the *Times* —
they rise, stretch full-length in the breeze like
any vacationer wanting a day in the sun, an even tan
to return with to a city, to proclaim "I too have been away."

Let us read. We can! Memory is our language. We are two
minds that lie athwart each other, two continental plates
with errant nationalities that articulate via subterranean grit.
In time, we will grind this world to powder, to be upraised
and bleached by processes of the seas.

But the wind blows. The surf ripples and slaps with the sough
of all the living and dead it has dissolved, and, with a great
respiratory suck, deposits on the beach what waves
must leave even as they take back what must be taken back.

Ah, you hear the anti-noise where gusts expose the sheet
of crumpled newsprint buried in the sand. What is written
is written. But we will lean close, intent, where
wind-blown grains pepper the page with faint pings.

*

It is one of those days when my will seems no more
than the will to conflate utter laziness with a poem
or with roiling sleepily in some good sex. Sleep,

O langorous sleep where I am forgetful of the misery
of history, my brutal West, a dozing Prince
before which all gives way.
                                    And summer

lightning at the sea's rim transforms the high
gorgeous blocks of clouds into a dance, a shadow-screen
of our imaginable gods: blue Buddha, Shiva of the knife,
Kali who follows footsteps in trackless sand, aerated Christ!

*

A weird pang of nameless joy. Look, a swimmer's head
is bobbing in the sea. And I point, my finger
like a sunbeam in a barrel. Here's this head

that moves from horizon to beach, this flesh-dot
that seems to swim away from the end
of an entrapping sentence, re-opening its syntax,

and so, for once, is at work against
premature closure. So I identify
a brother eidolon against the tide's flat reach.

*

Summer's paradise. Its rhythm. But not
the incessant flights of midges swarming in dark air,
alighting on the body through which hope and pain trickle,
those substantial rivers flowing to the seas.

Will you swat the tic of memory and enter into
ever-present babble of flies? Madness of the words.
Old tropes like brilliance of coral shoals on which
waves break and shipwrecks and glittery cabin lights
are extinguished in the deeps.

*

To the white sands who will speak a name?
The quiet of dusk comes back. Noiseless flight
of gulls inscribes the air and the world goes down
in a rhythm of deepening colors.

Surely the gods we invent bring out the night's phenomena:
flux into perfection, corollas and auroras, St. Elmo's fire
for all those who suffer the agonies of speech.

90

Objects, you
no longer offer up yourselves for ceaseless dictation,
no language anyway, our mouths are on each other.
Some lord of silence rises with stars and planets . . .

VI

IN THE MOUNTAINS, LINES OF CHINESE POETRY:

"the thread in the hand of a kind mother
is the coat on a wanderer's back"

Before she left this world, she stitched him tight.
Today, this mountain trail's her thread, on, up and out
to endless blue, and yet there's something unrelieved
about the space, his past, his childhood is
landscaped too. His fear for her, her damaged heart.

She slept on a throne-like bed at room's end
where he and his sister were not allowed to go.
He couldn't touch her, but, from where they stood,
he'd watch her sew. She was the view, but he was in it too.

Now his thoughts of her are like the bannered clouds
that float across the alpine grass, insubstantial
before the mountain's rock, hard otherworldly fact.
He would dream her back? Was she to inhabit every fear

and every wish? Eye-tug in mountain mist, he hoped,
in vacant, windblown heights, he'd find, not her, himself.
But it was only one improving stitch. She'd basted him, braided
thread right through his retina, her way itself defining sight.

BORN IN WATER

Born in water. I was born in
my mother's water and washed out
into the world from the burst sac.

When my mother died, we respected her wishes,
collected her ashes at the crematorium,
then spread them on the grass over my father's grave.

And because the wind was blowing,
we poured water from a plastic pitcher,
and added water from our eyes
so the ashes wouldn't blow away
but seep into the ground.

Mother and father, as on the day
I was conceived, mingled together.

PARTITIONS

The War

Lights out. The blackout curtains
Pushed aside. The moon was rising
Over hacked-off stumps of trees,

Limbs sawed away in the war's
Third year when the caterpillars
Came and went. We were sheltered

In our rooms, thrilled by the moon
Sailing down the river of backyards,
Over the chunky stumps, over roofs,

Chimney stacks and pots like sentinels
Against the starfilled night. Safe,
Safe for the moment;

The air of conflict,
A small boy's war on stoops.
Yet even then, neighbors were gone;

Flags hung behind glass. My father,
Just returned from an army camp,
Looked in, then went to my mother.

Out the window, stars too were distinct.
And suddenly, night was the greater heart
Vibrating knowledge not of death

But of loneliness: desire itself
To never again be fully quenched.

The Oath

> the vow/that makes a nation one body not be
> broken

— R O B E R T   D U N C A N

Was it only a few years ago
To have heard organ tones
Enlarge the fierce sad pomp?

Or was it when young. The weight
Of flag and anthem, *E pluribus unum*,
The nation upraised as god.

In the classroom, aged nine or ten,
Feeling aloneness, he had sung it,
"My country 'tis of thee..." he had sung

For apartness of his own,
A thrall which moved him
Toward company with others.

Yet why did he not hear the angry
Purpose, for which the falsehoods,
The fictions and tyrannies of war:

Parent coupled to the world,
The god-eye in that form,
Song set to receive it.

Was he not once the figure behind
Who longed and who ached,
Who did not know he moved in the falseness...

He could sing now on that theme
And find release. He could sing again
Inside.

He would hear first the childhood
And then the mockery, which entwined
As he thought the song must, gathering

So much for fear, so little
For love. Was this not the meaning
Of the note known for its own sake,

Was knowledge of the myth?

To hear the binding in which he stood,
Could stand so among the others
Who also sang:

In anthem once cojoined
The isolate man the child thought he was.

Street

Years later he would wake
As from a dream: had he
Grasped the elemental link?

The brownstone stoop
Piled against the brownstone house,
The way lives leaned on each other.

The horse-drawn cart
Was turning the corner
With its load of ice.

He followed with his mother
Watching the street weave and twist
In the great clear dripping blocks.

O how he wanted to let her hand go
And leap for chips and flakes
When the icepick struck, sending

Faultlines through
That mad bent imagery.

3:00 AM, *The Muse*

Not the power of speech
Nor the note blown into wholeness.
We seemed never to converse in the now as now.

What poetry there is
Is always late. Strange merely
To have thought. What

Rises out of what? Almost nothing
But this severe calm of identity.
I remember the animal moans:

The mute of that neighborhood
Of dusty laurels whom you released
From the locked-up movie house

Down the block. Young, beautiful.
Her cries startling us in the summer
Night. She had fallen asleep,

Only woke when the show ended
And the screen had gone dark for awhile.

MIAMI WATERS

Closing Up His Office Near the Ocean

Across the street
The bank clock winks *our* time
And the flat slabbed glass of walls
Catches knotted twists of light
Reflected off the ocean's waves
A few streets away.
                    Tossed in a black
Plastic trash bag: correspondence,
Scraps of old account books, stubs
Of receipts and checks.
Meanwhile, the sea
Recycles itself, holds what
Gives it its brackishness: the salt,
The inert, the living, the dead, swaying
In the one permeating taste.
                    In the office, not everything
Is thrown away. Brought back to the house
Will be photos and mementos, separated out
To supply the measured adequacy, the sharp flavor
Of earned sense. The rest could as well be left
Scattered on desk or floor
For the cleaning man to be puzzled by,
To pick over: some item overlooked,
A blank never filled, gain or loss,
Knowledge of which would end
In profit.
                    Now the mouth
Of the bag shows almost full.
Tied with a wire twist, it will gleam,
Black lump — not secrets but *minutiae* —
Under the florescent light
Like an unused altar in a corner.

At Biscayne Bay

Again, this year,
Palms suffer blight

But the luxurious green
Is elsewhere apparent

We take rides in rented cars.
Places you no longer visit,
Places fitfully recalled.

There's little looking and no talk.
Memories only intensify this sense
Of withering amidst profusion.

At last, we come to the bayside.
The paving runs into high grass

And the trees reach out, above
Where we used to fish. Dazzling

Underneath in sunlight and shade,
The current's one ineluctable:

Its constant change.

Aftermath

Waking to the sound of rain
In your house, almost a stranger's house,

I was reminded of years ago when
The storm's eye passed over the city

And left a violent harvest on the beach.
We kids went out, picked our way

Over fallen power lines, snapped trunks
Of trees, tongues of sand which reached up

Streets to cars and houses. Under grey skies
We marched gaily, survivors, to the ocean

Where among the bloated fish I found
A treasure, an ancient alarm clock propped

On sand. We played with it as in some dream
While offshore, the boats sprung loose

From their moorings tossed among the waves,
Spar and wreckage taking up the same wild motion.

St. Francis Hospital

A noise down the hall,
Another old man howls: "This is not my son,
This is not my daughter."

In the room, your eyes are wide,
Alert to what you think beyond you.

With part of you not here
(and not knowing where) we talk,
But conversation's not the proper word.

Someone has thoughtfully turned
The TV on above the bed,
The volume down.

It plays for benefit
Of nurse or visitor
Who at certain times must turn away.

In your head,
A Sybil rages,
Implodes together places, times, and years—

A text unbearable in its modernity.

Perhaps the world,
Which does not cohere in the world,
Coheres in one self, in one rememberer.

I think you want to tell me
One last time
That this is something shared

But your thoughts come almost
As another language. In the night
Outside, the arc lamps burn

And under the bridge the canal
Runs light and dark. The palms gleam
Like silvery feathers. I try to follow

Into the spillway of your words,
Meanings as loose upon the world
As this powdery effect of the light's particles.

FATHER STUDIES

I. *Bindweed*

Looking back to see you clear

The unkempt green clinging to the brick
You, framed against its swirls
There, in a sense, forever

How gripped in the child's equity
Equity of a weed and its twine
Toward flower

And the child, that delicate
Respectable bud

Following the light's trope
Bush, wall, petal, bug...
Not yet marking out a way of judging.

II. *Prophecy*

You too were born
Of a time and place

And now in the grey light
You sit avoiding blame

— All that you did not do
For yourself —

Avoiding what the flesh
Still wants to tell you

Complicity, complicity
Of reason gone to blame

As though we were all born

Owing blame, and whatever we did
Would barely change the story

"If you could see what I can see!"
I used to shout in my fear

When the light behind the blinds
Was like a seep of time

A millenium of light
Caught in the baffles

III. *History*

Such power you once had
To comfort and to hold

And now to find you
Weaker than myself

By that, think I wield
The power of your happiness

But promise and promise
Have gone to defeat

And the last defeat
Is unimaginable

The ghosts
Scattered now upon your eyes
Look back, *not out*

They emit a soundless howl
As they join
The century's conspirings

iv. *Whole Cloth*

Slats pulled, light blocked
Caught in whorls of random pattern

I know the sun blazes on the windows
At the room's far end

You sit upon the bed's edge
Shrunken, coiled over, as before
The altar of a vengeful god

And even now, the voice cracks
Remembering the vial's squeak
Upon the glass

Fear, and love which would save,
Complete the fabric

v. *Emergency's Furrow*

Sick, and the life narrowing
The road too clear ahead

Lost inside yourself, huddled
In an old striped robe, a tattered Joseph

I don't wonder that you commune
With the living and with the dead
— all are now your brothers

vi. *When*

When you were not there
I used to talk to the stuffed bear,
The wide-eyed doll

Their secret lives
I matched, adventure for adventure

Now all dreams become entwined
Terror with love, yours
With mine

Is this not the instruction:
The true life at last in the weave
Taking up the thread

THROUGH THE BINOCULARS

are the cranes returning to you
— HOLDERLIN

I.
White egret plumed against green grass
Great blue heron, these the first two
Noticed this year at the Point.

Heads dart under rushes for bright small fish,
For shells succulent with flesh: the movement
Of their beaks eats up and transposes time.

Air gusts off nearby flats. A moist wind
Carries the rot of split open shells; death
Scent and harbor scent, and the water's wide curl

Dark at the edge. And the wind tugs
Shadows at the birds' feet; sunlight
Scintillates and mazes at the lens.

This Mnemosyne loves: what distorts her weave
What the weave distorts in time.
And the birdbook too

Is almost an advisory: there are herons
That fail to migrate, remain in the North
When winter comes, and fall victims to severe weather.

And wasn't it only last week to have read
From the Chinese of the warrior who falls,
Who does not change, who has failed to submit

To the passage of the seasons. This summer,
Sic transit, my father has passed by. Overhead
A paper kite, a wind-bell's tinkle, and to think

An ear less to hear. Isn't this 'made up,'
That the father who has died has migrated.
Isn't this a changing of the season?

II.
Reeds shift in the wind, first gold
Then a dry silvery grey. Actually
The color they are cannot be grasped.

And the water throwing back its blue
Deepens shadows. What false power
Tries to posit two: observer and observed?

Something I observed is gone
And no ritual to perform
But a kind of letting go.

Thick rush of water
At the harbor's mouth; surely, it looked
This way last year. Yet I'm told

Unseen currents reclaim the old channels.
The heron dips its graceful head, claims
The fingerling in the time frame of the day.

III.
The day which also frames thoughts of cars
And people. That she borrowed the car,
Had trouble with the door, and the latch

Won't close, and by the tracks the car will sit
Unsecured. Years ago I moved away,
Had trouble with the locks. Yet this

Is less about what is taken or escapes,
Or even that the dead can't talk or have left.
This is only to say the dead will have released
All they will release.

IV.
Some herons remain beyond their time.
Some bright tasty thing at the water's edge
Overrides the migratory mechanism.

Bright things have claimed my new wife's time,
Have claimed mine as well. We tried in our times
To reclaim a season.

v.
A story: to send a letter
To his father dead in the pure land
Of Shambala. The son looks first

To the sun and the moon. Their light
Reaches, but they cannot deliver the letter.
He spies clouds passing lightly by, thinks

They can go there, but can they carry
The message? Birds fly overhead, going north;
These he appeals to without success. No one
But himself can deliver the message.

vi.
"are the cranes returning to you?"
Long lines fitted to elegies, strange hope
In constant repetition of word and phrase.

Or stand here. Binoculars make of the world
An eerie visitation: not only enlargement
But the coated lens' spectral hue. Odor of

Salt and sea pine, astringent as ancient myrtle.
How do you come to be here? With the twentieth
Century at your back. How does one lose the sense
Of the hymnic and must sing only of what is past?

vii.
In "harbinger" I heard the word "harbor" sound,
Found they both stem off an old French root...

As through the telescoping glass, a steady
Surface grain shows change: black-flecked rot
Of new leaf blight, the bleached red edge

Like a portent of the Fall. Look close.
New yellows can be confused with autumnal tones:
Harbingers. So that even the terms for seasons

Are a kind of babble. You can hear such confusion
In the language of the fathers as they fall
Through time. It sounds like hope haunting

The epochal voices which seek a stay against
Their time. *O keep me from this death*. Father,
All your words have died, yet, curiously, their muses

Live on. They hide here, in shadow
Between house and ground, or huddled by
The staved-in boat or by the daylily's stalk —

Wherever these birds gather and animate
What I write, telling me death too
Can be enlivened. The ear is a crypt.

VIII.
Of another poet. That the bird's feathers
"dangle down." Do you remember that phrase
From a time just past? Dead world. Dead poets.

I know someone who never met him
But called him father. Is there
Some residue to carry with this thought?

IX.
The breast of the heron close up
Is a maze of gnats. But think of the plumage
Of the dead. "*Tallis*, fresh underwear, black socks,
Bring these," scribbled on the funeral parlor envelope.

X.
You were here long after your time, here
And unable to care for yourself, unable
To talk, to know who had come into the room,

To remember what was said. How to keep such
Thoughts, which only a god or a presence
Is entitled to forget?

The mother, memory, has seen this cycle,
How the birds come back, how
The dead leaves are the new leaves' bed.

XI.
Look at the heron's feathers
Almost a shimmer in the wind or watch
Its nervous eye circuiting.

This is memory, this the message.

It is said the warrior's eyes ought to be sharp.
Perhaps he can foresee the onset of the seasons.
With binoculars, one sees further than one might.

XII.
Beautiful the world the dead have left us to see.
Beautiful the shell, thin and delicate in its own right,
Yet beautiful as a beautiful woman. Beautiful

The other isles where you lived and where the dead
Also go from, where palms fan out against the wind
And cruise ships studded with lights make way

Toward the sea, and the pelicans and gulls denied
To the dead follow behind. Beautiful this thought
Of the dead, the memory of the dead that follows

Like the waters out to the sea.
Is there some residue for the new season?

ON DRY LAKES TRAIL

Mother and father gone, and I, the new orphan,
new to my orphan-ness, summon what I can
to staunch the little gap.

For these rounds of my grief, I imported fauna
into the poem. For father, who died first,
the heron was imploded into lines and stanzas.
I thought of white-feathered Chinese death
and tic-like nervous beauty. So many times,
in his last years I saw him with his fingers
worrying his lower lip.

Mother, I played on reversals, the facts
of your life. You'd been cut by a dozen
operations, both breasts gone. And when,
by accident I found insurance photos
in an envelope amid the memorabilia,
I saw how the surgeon's knife had given
you the body of a male.

O miracle, that the force of you survived.
I saw it in that Bighorn ram at 12,000 feet
just above the Dry Lakes Trail, who pawed
and pawed at his succulent piece of turf,
flashed white battle scars in the brown fur
of his sides. I sensed the great warp
of distance by which you had to protect yourself.

High, high, high the reminders take me,
first against the sky, Horn Peak
to the right, Jane's photograph
catching you all silhouette, backlit
and black, authority and severity
flowing from you into horned isolate strength,
bone and space twisted on itself.
Yes, that was your grass, and it was we
who left, stumbling down the slope,
down to the trees and air, warmer air,

down to the path. But I hung back, Mother,
because of tears, hung back, as did you,
I walked home alone.

IN ELEGIACS, BIRDS OF FLORIDA

Gulls

Mother, those last vistas: you perched in the apartment which overlooked the wrinkled bay and the city whose patterned lights on the far shore resembled constellations. Near death, the whole world became a reading. So you too, father. At the home, I watched with you the palm fronds wave idly outside your room. Your eyes seemed to follow shadows on the walls, mind traceries, glints and powder darks, fan waverings of now and past, sea anemone, coral branch, yielding design but inarticulate.

Short stroll between you two, about the distance gulls will leave around a solitary walker who, at sunset, skirts the water's edge. A step too close either way and a gull will fly off, then another and another, to bob offshore on black water. Always a further horizon to inscribe a dividing line, a last blaze way out that catches the surf's turned edge. Before the salt nest of tombs, this consolation.

Flamingos

Are nearly a secret. Half gawk, half grace, their thin legs hold them unsteadily erect. They teeter on non-being. A flock, they move as one outlandish pink-feathered thought. Something like the mind's repository of hosts and legends, their passage through the world, the double helix's cosmic joke: herd, family, tribe—how dead shades in groups are driven across the universe.

Snowy Egrets and Herons

Are ubiquitous. They fish in the inland canals behind the great hotels or at bayside, near backyards and docks of pale white homes. I have seen them hang silently in trees, eye's gift, sacs of tissue-papered fruit, the kind one buys for funerals. At sunset, they march their young across the highways and the TaMiami Trail, their nests in sleepy willows and cypress. With the beat of their wings, they have made the Everglades the other side of Lethe. They roost too beside the airport, calm and self- involved, standing at runway's end in shallow puddles amidst their own reflections.

Mind Birds

With my son, sitting in the park in Miami after a trip to the Parrot Jungle, we conjured up invented birds: the Guantanamo Guano Dropping Bat, the Elixir Eider whose feathers could stuff waterbeds, the Woid Boid, the Brooklyn poet's finest fowl.

I imagine, too, the Memory Bird—O synapse that can scribe its following arc! It circles over these peopled beaches of Hades and Limbo like the fabulous Garuda, a bird which never lands nor rests. Such a creature is too expensive to feed or tame or bring to earth to lay its unblemished egg of certainty. Still, at its highest flights, its claws tear at one's heart and liver more viciously than the eagles of Prometheus.